It's All Mind

The Simplified Philosophy
of
A Course in Miracles

It's All Mind

The Simplified Philosophy
of
A Course in Miracles

By Edwin Navarro

It's All Mind: The Simplified Philosophy of A Course in Miracles
by Edwin Navarro
Copyright © 2010 by Edwin Navarro

Published by Edwin Navarro
www.edwinnavarro.com

First Edition: 2011

ISBN: 978-1456554965

Contents

Introduction

A Course In Miracles was written during the years 1965 to 1972 and was first published in 1976. The Course, as it will be referred to here, consists of three parts – a text, a manual for teachers, and a workbook for students, all totaling over 1000 pages. The text and the manual are to be read and studied, while the workbook consists of 365 daily lessons that provide a more direct experience and application of the ideas from the text.

The Course was written by Helen Schucman, a clinical psychologist who worked at several hospitals in New York. In describing how the Course was created, she refers to herself as a scribe, writing what came to her at different times of the day, always in a fully conscious state. She was able to stop the scribing process whenever she wanted and immediately return to it when she was ready. The author of the Course says he is Jesus, and it is written from the perspective of a teacher. For the full story of the creation of the Course, see Kenneth Wapnick's book 'Absence of Felicity'.

For the purposes of this book, the process of the creation of the Course is not important. What is important is the philosophy that grows out of the ideas in the text and how the application of that philosophy to our lives can result in fundamental changes in the way we see and experience the world around us.

For most people, the first experience of the Course is a difficult one for a number of reasons. First is the shear size and layout of the text, which was originally scribed in a continuous stream without sections or headings. These were added later to help in the organization of the ideas, but the 600+ pages of the text are still daunting for most.

Then there is the use of language. The Course is written in a semi-poetic form, at times more prose-like and at other times pure poetry. Words that have common meanings in Western thought take on different meanings in the Course. Much of the language of the Course sounds Christian in origin, but with careful study one realizes the terms are used in a new way. Biblical names, such as God, Jesus, Christ, and Holy Spirit all have different meanings from the way they are used in the Bible. Other terms from the Bible, such as sin, atonement, forgiveness, and miracle are also used differently.

The Course is really a combination of a spiritual and a psychological text. There are common terms, some from psychology, which are also used in a unique way, such as ego, separation, projection, and special. While reading the Course one has to be careful to be open to these meanings and not to project one's preconceived ideas onto it. In addition to the difficulty of the language, understanding the concepts within the language can be very challenging. Often people will read a few paragraphs or a couple of pages at a time and need to set it down for a while to think about it.

There have been many books written about the Course, and they tend to follow two general lines of development. In one, short quotes are taken from the Course and from these quotes general ideas related to everyday living are developed. They usually fall into the category of self-help books, and many of them can be helpful for people looking to change relationships in their lives.

The second category of books is more focused on explanations of the Course, with long passages from the text that are examined and explained using more accessible language. Often they include extensive definitions of terms used in the Course, especially where these definitions are different from common usage. These books can be helpful when used in conjunction with study of the text and when following the lessons in the workbook.

So why another book about *A Course In Miracles?* The purpose of this book is different from either of those just mentioned. The goal here is to use the basic concepts from the Course to build a simple, consistent philosophy in the format of a short book. The hope is that such a book can aid those who are trying to understand the Course better and also be useful as an everyday guide toward seeing the world differently and making changes in how one interacts with the world.

The philosophy begins with some basic assumptions about the nature of God and the Natural State of Being. From these assumptions the development will follow logical steps to show how the world we experience came into being and how we have chosen to interact with that world. Finally the philosophy will show us how we can move beyond the negative experience of our lives and re-experience our Natural State of Peace within a Loving God.

God

There is a quote from the Course, "We say 'God is,' and then we cease to speak..." From a pure experience point of view, this is all that needs to be said. The True God of *A Course in Miracles* is Pure Oneness and cannot be described using our dualistic point of view and language. However, in order to understand the experience of our everyday world, the Course and this philosophy need to talk about God from a dualistic point of view at times – describing what God is like and what God is not like.

Our goal is to use our language to describe God in a way that is as close to reality as we can, knowing we will never completely describe the True God. As we develop the philosophy we will find this dualistic way of viewing God is ultimately illusory, but for now we need to understand how the world we experience came to be.

There are many descriptive statements that might be made about God, but it will be sufficient for this development to consider the following four aspects of God.

1 - God is All That Is, Everything. There is nothing that is not God.

2 - God is Mind, Thoughts, Ideas and nothing but Mind.

3 - God is Pure Love. All experiences of God are Loving.

4 - God Creates. God is not static, but is in a constant state of Creating.

If there were complete acceptance and belief in these four aspects, there would be no need for the Course. The purpose of the Course is to help us discover the barriers that prevent us from believing these ideas and to teach us how to remove those barriers.

1 – God is All That Is, Everything

Rather than just being omnipresent, in this philosophy God *is* everything. We are God and everything we think, feel, experience, observe, etc. is God. Nothing exists outside of God. If we believe we are experiencing something that is not God, we are simply fooling ourselves. Specifically this means the belief we are bodies or souls living in this world, and God is an entity outside of us, is an illusion.

2 – God is Mind

One of the more radical concepts in this philosophy is that God is only Mind. Anything we experience is an idea in the Mind of God, and since only Mind is real, anything material, physical, corporeal, etc. must be an illusion, only an idea. The entire physical world with all of its complexity is just an illusory thought, and if we believe something is solid, permanent, or objective, we are deluding ourselves. In this philosophy everything happens in our minds, and any change we want to see must take place in our minds.

3 – God is Pure Love

In our world it is difficult to imagine an experience of Pure Love, but it is fundamental to the philosophy that God is only Love. If we think we are experiencing a God that is in any way less than a Loving God, then that 'God' is another illusion. We will see how in this philosophy one of the barriers to the experience of God is to see a 'God' that is not Loving. A 'God' that is judgmental, punishing, or merely too remote and abstract to experience is not a Loving God and must be illusory.

4 – God Creates

It is important not to see God as a static experience. God is the Source of our being – we are God's creations, and this creation takes place in the Mind of God, which is the only place it can happen. Once created, we are fundamentally co-creators extending the experience of God. Those creations occur in our minds and therefore only exist and are only experienced in our minds, which are ultimately in the Mind of God.

There are a number of immediate conclusions that can be drawn from these four aspects of God. If everything is Mind, what we experience as a body living in a physical space and time must be an illusion, and in essence we have fooled ourselves into believing in an external material world. Since God is All-Loving, the whole idea of a vengeful 'God' or a judgmental 'God' must also be an illusion. Both of these ideas fly in the face of our experience and in the face of most established religions.

So why do we experience in our everyday lives something so different from this Natural State of Being? How is it possible we experience something other than Love? How can we possibly experience pain and attack or guilt and fear? All of these can be traced to our belief in the idea of separation.

The Idea of Separation

Having described the four aspects of God, we are now looking for a logical development that will lead us to better understand how we got to our current state of being from our Natural State. It is only necessary to find a single such development that can describe our current experience. The key fact is all of this is taking place within the Mind, which allows for great freedom.

Suppose for a moment there was a thought of being separate from God. If the Mind of God *is* Everything, how can the thought of being separate from God exist? Since God is Creative, any thoughts are possible and free to be explored, so in some small corner, the illusory thought of separation is possible. But can a part of God's Mind actually separate from the Mind of God? In reality it cannot, but that does not mean the idea of separation and all of the possibilities it would entail cannot be explored. This is where we find ourselves.

Once the thought of separation occurs, the next question is, How would such a separation manifest itself and what would the experience be like? The first realization is that in order for any part of God to believe it has separated from God, it must delude itself, since real separation is impossible. How might such a delusion be formed?

Denying God

First the experience of God would have to be avoided, since this would break the spell of the belief in separation. One way to do this would be to introduce the idea of fear and the idea of something to be feared. In this scenario, God would become the focus of the fear; for if we do not fear God and were to re-experience the God of Pure Love, the illusion of separation would fall apart.

One way to create a fear of God is to see this new 'God' as an enemy who is out to harm us in some way, perhaps by judging us and potentially wanting to punish us for what we have done. This may sound preposterous, since God, by definition is Pure Love, but it shows how absurd the idea of separation is and how much must be done to prop it up. If God were considered a friendly presence, the attraction to re-experience the Loving God would be too strong.

The Separated Self

So an illusion has been created that essentially creates a ring around a portion of those thoughts of separation. Within that ring, all the thoughts are focused on seeing what is outside the ring as dangerous and fearful – an enemy. To reiterate, the ring, the fear, the enemy, are all imagined and have no basis in truth, and they can only maintain their illusory state by constant effort to see something that is not there. The thoughts within that ring we will call the separated self.

Now suppose this scenario has been played out and a new separated self has been created. Of course, there really is no separated self, but there is a belief it has been created. This self will live in a state of fear, loneliness, and guilt for having cut itself off from what was its Natural Loving State of Being.

This state creates a great tension between the misery of the separated state and the nearness of God. The separated self will want to distance itself from this misery by building new barriers, new thoughts and ideas to focus on that will help it forget its true Natural State. One way the self can do this is to create within the ring the illusion of a separate external world, onto which it can project all of its guilt, pain, and fear.

The Separate External World

This external world is another construct of ideas, but the separated self can now believe it is real, a place where the self sees attacks occurring, along with pain and fear. Of course, all of this pain is being projected by the self onto the world, and then being perceived as external to the self. The delusion grows as the separated self tries to build new barriers to the experience of God.

At this point the separated self can now create the illusion of countless other separated selves, all existing in this projected world, and all interacting with one another, all projecting their thoughts out onto the world. The self can now be free of responsibility for the original thought of separation and allow the blame to be externalized. This has the additional benefit of creating a further layer of separation from God and the experience of Love.

The separated self can see itself as a lone bit of sanity in an insane external world – a world where the experience of love is fleeting, where death is always waiting, where attack, whether physical or emotional, is always present. By focusing on this world and learning how to defend itself from all these attacks, the memory of the Natural State fades further away. Of course, all of this is one great illusion – this separated self has never left God – but it will do what it must to maintain the idea of separation.

Since the separated self has created the external world to be a place of fear and attack, whenever this self interacts with this world, it will experience exactly what it projects onto that world. As the self further learns to project and then interact with the world, it begins to see the external world as its home. It becomes dependent on that world for its life and its sustenance. It begins to build up defenses to the attacks that are, by definition, part of that world – the world that is a completely delusional projection.

The Ego

So now a separated self has been created. That self initially denied God in order to experience separation, and the denial led to the experience of guilt and fear. In order to free itself from some of this guilt and fear and in order to increase the illusion of separation, this self projected within the ring an external world that will contain all the same guilt, fear, pain, and attack that the separated self experiences. That world becomes the home in which the self believes it exists, which means a delusional self is living in an imaginary world.

When discussing this separated self, it is important to understand that this self does not represent a person or a soul or any other of our common ideas of what a self is. Here the separated self is simply a construct of illusions that created the ring that separates these thoughts from the Oneness of the true Mind of God. The ring is not real and the idea of a separated self that can experience pain and guilt and fear is not real. But for the separated self, the illusion seems real, the external world seems real, and the pain and guilt and fear seem real. For the remainder of the discussion, we will refer to the part of the separated self that focuses on maintaining the separation as the 'ego'. Later we will find there is another part of this separated self that has never left its Source and offers an alternative to the ego.

The Ego

The ego is the part of the separated self that focuses solely on the maintenance of the belief in separation. So what methods might the ego use to further the sense of separation and aloneness of the separated self? Most importantly, the ego must use whatever it can, especially guilt and fear, to prevent the separated self from remembering its connection to God. One of the ways it can maintain this belief is to try to keep the separated self focused on a separate external world. This creates a constant distraction for the self observing all the activity, attack, pain, and death that is a part of that world.

The ego can also create the illusion of a body to further emphasize the separation and individuality of the self. These mental actions keep the ego in charge and God hidden away, and though it all sounds very depressing and futile, remember the ego is just another illusory part of the illusory separated self that has never truly left the Mind of God. We explore the ego here in order to understand how it works and how we can free ourselves of its hold on us.

The External World

We have talked about the concept of the separated self and discussed the fact that there is no self that was created, but only a construct of ideas. One of the ego's goals is to create a solid feeling of self, of being an isolated individual living in an external objective world. The external world we experience is a projection of the ego. The ego imagines guilt, fear, and attack and then creates a complete external world that contains all of the same guilt, fear, and attack.

The self then perceives this world as external and must use its focus and energies interacting with this world as if it was completely separate, when in reality it is all its own projection. As long as the self believes this world is separate, it will fail to realize how it has been deluded absolutely by the ego. The people we interact with, nature in all of its power and uncertainty, our activities, jobs, and creative work are all part of this ego construction. In order to interact with this projected world, the ego takes it one step further and constructs and maintains the illusion of a body.

The Body

As part of this illusion the ego creates a body with a precise sense of inside and outside. Within the body we appear to be at the mercy of our internal metabolic processes while from outside the body we are at the mercy of external forces. We spend, at the ego's request, a tremendous amount of our time building up defenses for our bodies. We build houses and other spaces to live, work, and play in. We procure and prepare sustenance for our bodies, and if we do not eat the right foods or exercise right, we feel guilty about what we might be doing to our bodies. The goal is to prolong the body in what we define (really what the ego defines) as a healthy state.

But lurking in our future is some kind of sickness, and that sickness may be generated internally in the body or it may be the result of some external agent that causes the sickness. Once we are sick, we must find external solutions to combat the sickness, and the ego tells us if we just take the right medicine or have the particular surgery or other procedure, we can return our bodies to health. Once again we turn over to the ego the power to make us whole, since we have been sold an illusion of a body living in an illusory world that now has an imagined illness, and to cure ourselves we look to the biggest illusion of all, the ego. And when we are old or too sick to keep our bodies going, we believe death will be the final chapter.

The Idea of Death

The ego has created an even greater idea to focus the energies of the self away from God – the idea of death. Everyone learns from an early age that their bodies and other bodies are all going to die eventually. Our societies exert great effort and resources to prolong the life of the body to put off death as long as possible. But we also know death could occur in the next instant, and therefore we as bodies are never secure in this world. Given that experience, how could we imagine there was a Loving God who put us and our bodies in this world? The reality is none of this exists in any objective way.

Then what is death? The answer lies in understanding what it is that is dying. When we examine human death, the only thing we are sure is dying is the human body. But the body is a creation of the ego, which is a part of the separated self. So the death of a body is only the death of an illusion – an illusion the ego has created to try to trap the separated self in this external world. In our philosophy the Mind of God is eternal, and so is any conceivable part of the Mind of God, so no matter how compelling it may seem, death is just another illusion created by the ego.

There is a line in the Course, 'We leave this world not by death, but by Truth.' If we are separated selves living within the Mind of God, then the death of the body is simply an illusory act (death) on an illusory object (the body), and therefore the death of the body does not free us from the separation. Only the Truth of our Existence in God can finally free us from our belief that we are separated selves.

Hiding From God

As was mentioned, it is essential to the ego that we do not re-experience our existence within the Mind of God. God must be feared and we must feel deep guilt about our fear of God. There are basically two belief systems that exist in our world. One denies the existence of God, and for those who believe this, the world is a place of chance and chaos. One never knows what nature may inflict upon the self in this world – earthquakes, job loss, a car accident, loss of a friend, or perhaps the asteroid that hits the earth. This means the self must be in a constant state of fear. The fear may be deeply hidden and the external personality may be bright, but the ego-driven actions the self takes will be centered on how to maintain the body in this uncertain world.

The second basic belief, which pervades almost all religions to some extent, is the idea of God as a judgmental entity. In this scenario there is usually a concept of a life after death, and what that life is like is a result of what we do while we are here. Once again the ego creates a 'God' that is not Pure Love and we must be in fear of that 'God' because our future is in its hands. Since we can never live the life completely that we are told we should (told by the ego, of course), we are constantly feeling guilty knowing we are offending this 'God'.

In both of these scenarios, the True God is hidden, and the fact this whole construction is a total illusion is obscured. If we can just go back to before the separation, there was and is nothing but the Mind of God, and all of the ego's manipulations are focused on maintaining the forgetting. As we will see later, there are ways to start to remember who and what we really are, ways that will ignore what the ego tells us is true and allow us to begin to see what is really there.

Judgment

Another tool the ego uses to focus the separated self on the external world is judgment. When we see this world from the ego's dualistic point of view, we are constantly judging the experiences, people, and ideas of this world. Fundamentally everything is looked at as to whether it increases pain or pleasure, and the mere process of judging means we have accepted the dualism of the ego. Thus judgment helps to perpetuate the ego.

When we interact with people, we use judgment constantly to determine who can be our friends, who shares our politics, who we can love, who we can hate, who we need to fear. As we do this we place people in specific categories and by so doing we separate some people from others, leading to a strengthening of the idea of separation. The ego wants us to judge others and it also wants us to fear judgment from others. Through this process we lock ourselves deeper into this illusory world.

Special Relationships

As an extension of the idea of the ego, there is a concept in the Course of special relationships. These relationships are considered special because these are the ones we focus on and tend to perpetuate, sometimes for most of our lives. Special relationships are broadly categorized into special hate and special love relationships. The use of the word hate may seem strong, but in the Course, anything not Loving is not of God, so the word hate is used for all non-Loving experiences. Special love relationships are based on an ego definition of what love is, but in reality the two types are one and the same. Though special relationships can be broadly defined to be in relation to anything in the external world, we will focus on relationships with people here.

Special hate relationships are with those we feel we must attack or with those we perceive as attacking us. This may be very personal, with family members, for instance, or they may be more remote, perhaps toward political figures or criminals. Here we use the word attack to mean any desire to see the other person experience more pain, whether physical, emotional, etc. Perceiving others attacking us leads us to build up defenses to those attacks. In the broadest sense this includes military defense of our territory, and in a more personal case it may lead us to try to avoid interaction with another person out of fear. It also provides our ego selves with justification for attacking back at anyone who we believe is trying to do us harm. It's all part of the great ego illusion, of course, since it was the ego who projected the world of attack outward for us so we could perceive it.

Special love relationships are a bit more subtle but just as ego-driven as the hate relationships. These are defined as those relationships where we are looking for something to fulfill ourselves and we form an external relationship to satisfy that need. These can be parent-children, spouses, close friends, etc. Usually these relationships start out happy and over time seem to lose some of their luster. The reason for the degradation is that the other party in the relationship is being used to satisfy the first party's needs. When this becomes more evident, the relationship either needs to evolve beyond the special category, or it will either break up or go on as a dependent and maybe not so loving relationship.

When we build special relationships in our life, we are once again providing the ego with just what it wants – more attention on the external world. As with everything the ego does, the first step is for us to recognize the special relationships in our lives. As we look at those special hate relationships where we seem to be unable to ever let them go, and the special love relationships that never fulfilled our expectations, we can become more aware of how the ego has fooled us into believing these were so important.

There are two fundamental lessons the Course tries to teach us. The first is to recognize how the ego operates in our lives as it projects onto the world all of our internal guilt, fear, and pain. In recognizing the actions of the ego, we begin to see the barriers that prevent us from experiencing the Love of God. The second lesson is to learn how to break through those barriers through the practice of forgiveness.

Forgiveness

In this development we started with the four aspects of God. We then explored how a world like our current experience might have evolved, which led to the concept of separation, a mental construct of illusory ideas. We defined that ringed off set of ideas as the separated self, and the ego as the portion of the separated self focused on maintaining the separation. We examined how the ego creates the illusion of our separate external world, with our bodies inhabiting that world, and the many ways the ego maintains the illusion.

We now want to look at the part of the separated self that remembers its Natural State within the Mind of God. The ego wants to suppress that memory any way it can, but the memory is there nonetheless. The Course offers us the idea of forgiveness as our way to break the hold of the ego and to let the memory come to the surface. By forgiving the world we perceive, we will begin the path back to God.

The Definition of Forgiveness

In common usage forgiveness means to give up resentment toward someone or something. The word is used often in Christian thought, but can also be used as a psychological term. In either case the resentment is seen as detrimental, and forgiveness will free us from those feelings. The term is most often used in regard to forgiving another person for some attack on oneself, whether physical, psychological, or emotional. In any case the assumption is the attack did occur and you are simply letting go of your resentment toward the person who attacked you.

In the Course, forgiveness has a very different and specific meaning and a unique power. Remember we began with our True Existence in the Mind of God. All else is illusion, including the separated self and the world in which that self believes it is living. If this is all an illusion then any attack on this self must be an illusion as well. The ego wants us to see the attack as real, but if we can realize it is an illusion, the attack has no power against the self. This is what is meant by forgiveness in the Course – realizing the attack never really happened. In essence we forgive our perception of the event, which by extension forgives the person as well. Remember the ego has projected the world we perceive, so as we forgive the world around us, we weaken the power of the ego.

An Example of Forgiveness

As an example, suppose a person, let's call him John, is out on the street and someone, who we'll call Fred, threatens him with a weapon and robs him of all his valuables. John will find this to be an upsetting and fearful experience, and he has now developed a special hate relationship with Fred. Suppose Fred is later caught and John meets up with him. In the common usage of the idea of forgiveness, if John wants to forgive Fred and give up his resentment, he might say, "I know you did something awful and it upset me very much, but I forgive you for what you did to me, because I'm trying to be a better person."

In this common way of forgiveness, John's motivation may be to be a better Christian or just a better person in some way, but he still believes the original robbery (attack) occurred. He has forgiven the person, but has not rethought the experience. Therefore he is in the same place of fearing that another attack could occur, and because of the first attack, he will likely be more fearful of another attack. So the ego has really won by maintaining the fear of the separate external world.

With the concept of forgiveness in the Course, something quite different occurs. Instead of John forgiving Fred, John is really forgiving the *experience* of the robbery. He realizes that, contrary to what the ego is telling him, Fred and all others in this world are part of the same Mind of God, and any attack he perceives has first been projected outward by his ego, and then perceived by him as an external attack.

This may at first be quite difficult for him to realize, but if he is working with the Course and trying to apply the concepts, he knows the only way to counter the ego is to learn this means of forgiveness. In this scenario the ego has been weakened, because the ego is dependent on the separated self seeing external attacks. If John begins to realize these attacks are not external, but projected by his ego, then the ego cannot be in charge.

No Degrees of Attack

It is important to realize the word attack is used in a very general sense and there are no degrees of attack. Being physically attacked is just the same as someone saying an unkind word about you, or a politician wanting to raise your taxes or take away your benefits, or your boss demanding something from you. In all these cases the ego has projected an experience that is not perceived as Loving, and in all these cases forgiveness can free your perception of the experience and allow you to realize the ego was fooling you again. It doesn't matter where you begin your forgiveness, it only matters that you apply it to everything. If you withhold forgiveness for any one thing, the ego has maintained its illusion of separation.

This generality of attack is also true with regard to time. There is a correlation between the concepts of attack (inflicting pain), guilt, and fear, and the concepts of past, present, and future. Attacks relate to events that once they have occurred are in the past. Guilt is experienced in the present about some act from the past. And fear relates to something bad that may occur in the future. As with the different types of attack, it is also important to apply forgiveness to all times of attack. You should forgive illusions of attack from decades ago as well as ones from minutes ago. Guilt about past acts should be forgiven equally, and fears about possible attacks in the future should also be forgiven. The time of the attack does not matter – just do not withhold forgiveness for any perceived attack.

The Holy Spirit

Of course it's not always going to be easy to forgive. The mere fact we perceive ourselves as bodies living in an external world means we have given a great deal of power to the ego, whose sole reason for being is to maintain the separation. We said earlier there is another part of the separated self that remembers its existence within the Mind of God. The Course refers to this part as the Holy Spirit.

The term Holy Spirit clearly has a Christian origin, but as with many ideas in the Course, the definition is very different. It really makes no difference what we call this part of the separated self – the Self That Remembers, the Inner Voice, the Inner Guide – what is important is the meaning. So we will use the term Holy Spirit here to be consistent with the Course, but you might decide to use a different name if it more readily connects you to the meaning.

The Holy Spirit and Forgiveness

The Holy Spirit might be seen within our minds as a personality or a larger than life spiritual entity. We envision this entity as being the part that remembers our True Existence. The process of forgiving an attack starts with recognizing we have perceived an attack occurring in the external world. We then take that attack, and knowing that to the Holy Spirit the attack could never have occurred, we hand off to the Holy Spirit all of our feelings about the attack, and by doing so we free ourselves of these feelings.

A more visual and less personal way to think of the Holy Spirit is as a tunnel that opens out from the ego's world through the ego's barriers and through the outer ring into the True Mind of God. It's a mental path through which we access our Natural State. By envisioning this tunnel we can again hand off the pain, guilt, and fear that we experience in the ego's world, so it can be sucked into that tunnel to disappear into the Mind of God. What is happening when we do this is we are for a brief moment remembering where we came from, and by doing so we are forgiving the experience which led to our feelings of attack.

So now let us return to our example of John and Fred. If John is trying to forgive the robbery (attack) that he perceived, he will apply the concepts of the Course by first realizing the attack is just a projection of his own ego. He will then take the experience with all of the negative feelings associated with it and hand it off to the Holy Spirit. By doing so he will for a brief moment remember his True Existence, and in that moment the ego will no longer be in charge. The attack will be seen for the illusion it is, and John will have freed himself a bit more from the oppression of the ego.

What Else Can We Forgive?

We have been focusing on forgiveness in the context of forgiving another person for a perceived attack. When we use the method of forgiveness from the Course, we are really forgiving the experience of the attack. By extension the person who we believed attacked us in the first place is also forgiven, since if the attack did not occur, the person did not commit the attack.

We can extend this idea of forgiveness to internal guilts about acts we believe we have committed in the past, illnesses that may appear to have come from within the body or from an outside agent, the fears we have about attacks that could occur in the future, and our judgments and the judgments of others. And of course there is also the fear and guilt we feel about our initial rejection of the Loving God and our replacement with the ego's concept of the judgmental 'God' or the non-existent God.

Guilt and Sickness

In the case of guilt, we feel bad in the present about some act we believe we committed in the past that inflicted pain in some way. We can forgive ourselves by forgiving the act, since whatever we believe occurred was a projection of our ego and therefore an illusion. We can hand off to the Holy Spirit all of the negative feelings we carry with us about what we believe we did. By doing so we briefly remember our True Existence, and the ego projections and the associated feelings fade away.

As long as we believe we are bodies living in an external world, our bodies will experience illnesses at times. These may be serious, like cancer or heart disease, or they may be ordinary, like a cold or strained muscles. In any case the illness must be an illusion since the body is an illusion. The illness is caused by the ego trying any way it can to get the separated self to focus more on the body. To forgive the illness, we first realize that the body and the illness are illusions and then we pass to the Holy Spirit all the negative feelings we have from the illness. We allow the remembrance of our Natural State to heal the illusion we believed in.

Fear and Judgment

Fear relates to events that have not yet occurred. They may relate to a personal attack, to getting sick, to a natural catastrophe – essentially to any kind of event that could occur that would cause pain to the self. Since these haven't occurred, they are already known to be illusions to the self. In this case we hand off all those future illusions with our feelings of fear about them to the Holy Spirit. It is possible to live without fear, but it requires constant vigilance to forgive any new fears the ego may try to project.

The judgments we place on this world, and the fear of judgment from the world, help to perpetuate the power of the ego, and these judgments lock us in to the ego's dualistic view of the world. We first must realize the process through which we place people and experiences into different categories is another illusion. There are no differences, only the illusion of difference. As we start to judge someone, we should invoke our experience of the Holy Spirit and pass to the Holy Spirit the judgment we are about to make, and through this we will for the moment remember our True State where judgment does not exist. The illusion of the categories will fade a bit more. We can use this same process when we perceive judgment from others.

Guilt and Fear of God

Some of the deepest fears and guilts we experience are related to our feelings about God. Remember the whole idea of separation started with our rejection of the Loving God and the creation of a judgmental, punishing 'God', or the belief there is no God. In either case we have substituted our Loving place in the Mind of God with a non-Loving experience in this world, which has led to deep pain, guilt, and fear. We must forgive our guilt for believing we left God and our fear of some kind of retribution from the judgmental 'God'. The Holy Spirit stands ready to help us heal those feelings as well. First we must recognize our part in creating this illusion and then release those feelings to the Holy Spirit to remember again our Existence in the Loving Mind of God.

The Way Home

We began our philosophy with the four aspects of God. These aspects define our Natural State of Being. Then the idea of separation occurred, which is just an illusion, but the idea led to the ringed off separated self, another illusion. We defined the ego as the part of the separated self that maintains the illusion of separation. We explored the different ways the ego works to maintain that illusion. We then learned about forgiveness and how through forgiveness we can begin to break the hold of the ego. With the help of the Holy Spirit, the part of the separated self that remembers its Natural State, we free ourselves of the pain, guilt, and fear in our lives.

The first part of the development of the philosophy is focused on understanding how we got where we are and how we maintain our current separated state. Through this understanding we can begin to recognize the actions of the ego. Once recognition has occurred, we begin to forgive all the attacks at all different levels in our lives. Through this process of forgiveness, we are letting go, step by step, of the separation illusion, and we will remember more and more our Natural Existence in the Mind of God.

Peace

So where does all of this lead? The stated goal in the Course is to experience Peace. What does Peace mean in the Course? In essence it is a state of continual forgiveness, living your life with a constant realization the world we inhabit is an illusion and is not our True Home. As events occur, they are instantly seen as illusions, instantly forgiven, and any negative feelings are passed on to the Holy Spirit. By continually forgiving our experiences in this world, the ego is no longer in charge of the separated self. The pain, guilt, and fear that are normally experienced are forgiven and this new self identifies more and more with the Holy Spirit. The remembrance of our True Natural State becomes ever stronger.

How can we experience this Peace? As with many things we learn in this world, through constant practice. The ego is a strong force and before coming to the Course we spent much of our lives believing the ego's view of the world, a place of fear and attack from which we must protect ourselves. Once we open ourselves to an awareness of the Holy Spirit's presence, we can begin the process of breaking down all of the ego's barriers – all of the guilt and fear we have accepted from the ego throughout our lives.

Through the experience of the Holy Spirit, we can begin to remember on a daily basis our True Existence in the Mind of God. Eventually that daily remembrance can become a constant remembrance and a state of continual forgiveness can be achieved. Peace can be ours whether our bodies continue to inhabit this world or not.

How long will all of this take? The Course talks about time in many different ways and from different perspectives. From some perspectives it may seem to take eons, from others it seems only an instant. But the bottom line is this – It doesn't really matter. As long as we are clear in our intent, as long as we know what the ego is doing, as long as we turn to the Holy Spirit, we are promised we will find our way back Home.

As we experience Peace in our lives and realize the attacks we perceive are not real, we will naturally become more kind to others. Through the practice of kindness we help to further weaken the hold of the ego. We begin to see others as more like us and we begin to recognize the kindnesses that naturally happen in the world, but are normally blocked from our view by the ego. Once Peace becomes our everyday experience and kindness is a constant practice, there is nothing in the world that can take this from us. Our Peace is our own and any attack on that Peace is just a fleeting illusion that will instantly die away.

The End of Illusion

There will come a time when this world of illusion and separation will be gone. Everything we currently experience – past, present, and future – will disappear. Once we find our way back to the Loving Mind of God, all of the illusions that have grabbed our focus will fade away. The separated self and the ring that encloses it, the ego and all of its tricks, our external world and all of the bodies in that world, even the Holy Spirit who helped lead us out of the illusion – all of these will be gone and we will live in a state of Love and Peace unimaginable to us where we are now.

So focus now on the end of the illusion. Learn the subtle ways the ego holds you to this world, and begin to forgive the experiences in your life. Turn to the Holy Spirit for help in releasing your pain, guilt, and fear, and practice every day toward the goal of continual forgiveness. The end of illusion is guaranteed. Maintain your intent and know that as Peace grows within us, our place within the Loving Mind of God is assured.

God Again

Now the four aspects collapse into none,
For God cannot be parsed.

The ring has melted away,
For there is nothing left to separate.

The ego has evaporated,
Only a lost cruel joke.

Forgiveness is gone,
For there is nothing left to forgive.

The Holy Spirit is free,
Our Remembered Friend led us Home.

The separated self has rejoined,
Back into its Natural Loving State.

Now.

We Are.

God Is.

Suggested Reading

A Course in Miracles, Second Edition, Foundation for Inner Peace, www.acim.org

Wapnick, Kenneth, *The Message of A Course in Miracles, Vol. 1, All Are Called*, Foundation for *A Course in Miracles*, www.facim.org

Wapnick, Kenneth, *Absence from Felicity*, Foundation for *A Course in Miracles*, www.facim.org

Excerpts from *A Course in Miracles* copyright 1975, 1992, 1999 by Foundation for *A Course in Miracles*.

Contact the author at www.edwinnavarro.com

13366267R00026

Made in the USA
Lexington, KY
27 January 2012